The ULTIMATE LinkedIn Profile Template

*Get the **EXACT** words, phrases and **formatting hacks** that turn your **LinkedIn Profile** into a **lead-generating, client-attracting piece of content!***

John **Nemo**

Bestselling LinkedIn Author, Trainer & Speaker

I want to start with some encouraging news.

I've built a 7 figure business exclusively from clients I've found on LinkedIn.

And yet this is me on most days:

Also, I dress like this:

And this:

My point: If *this* guy can build a 7 figure business from LinkedIn, what's *your* excuse?!

Yes, I have the worst fashion sense on the planet.

Yes, my poor wife proves daily that love is truly blind.

And yes, I've built a 7 figure business from clients I've found on LinkedIn.

How It Happened

Quick story: I quit a safe, 6 figure day job back in 2012 with one client, enough money for 30 days, 3 boys under the age of 10 and my wife (who had quit her job to come home and take care of the boys) all counting on me.

Naturally, it was the *perfect* way to launch a new business.

I opened my digital marketing agency (Nemo Media Group) with no budget and no investors.

In fact, here's a look at my first "office" in the corner of our bedroom –

Yes, that's a soft pretzel box that I perched my laptop on!

Now, before you think I'm *totally* nuts, I knew what I was doing.

Even back in 2012, I'd seen something with LinkedIn - that it could be *so* much more than just a "jobs" platform.

So I started using LinkedIn from Day 1 as my go to place to find new clients.

And, within 90 days, I'd generated $135,000 of revenue - all from clients I found on LinkedIn.

And I got to spend my days at the "office" doing this –

That crazy journey led to me being featured in and guest blogging for:

• American City Business Journals
• Business Insider
• Entrepreneur On Fire
• Inc. Magazine
• LinkedIn's Official Marketing Blog
• Social Media Examiner

Over the past decade, I've helped countless Business Coaches, Consultants and Small Business Owners land 5-6 figure clients using LinkedIn:

I've generated over $50,000 in new business as a direct result what I learned inside the LinkedIn Riches Premium Training. When it comes to LinkedIn, John Nemo is a rock star!

John Hawkins, Executive Coach, Consultant & Speaker

Just secured a $30,000 client using what I discovered inside of LinkedIn Riches ... thank you John!

Mark McGraw, Sandler Sales Training

I took John's training, implemented what I learned on LinkedIn, and immediately added a $24,000 recurring yearly client!

Paramita Bhattacharya, Small Business Owner

Within 60 days of investing in LinkedIn Riches, I'd landed a high-level client for an ongoing, $7,500 monthly retainer, along with several other new clients at different tiers of my various coaching and consulting programs. I also have a backlog of new prospects wanting to sign up for my programs, so much so that I've actually had to dial back my lead generation efforts on LinkedIn. John's system is working TOO well!

Bill Prater, Executive Coach & Consultant

Bottom line: I can attribute over $20,000 in new revenue to my LinkedIn activity based on your LinkedIn Riches program insights. I have another $10,000 in outstanding proposals that I feel confident will land in the next few weeks. There is not a week that goes past when I do not have new leads generated from my continuing to follow this program's advice!

Paul Copcutt, Branding & Marketing Consultant

(You can <u>read and see more testimonials</u> here.)

I've also *personally* rewritten LinkedIn profiles for A-List Entrepreneurs, Speakers and Bestselling Authors including:

- Bob Burg
- Chris Brogan
- Dan Miller
- Jairek Robbins
- John Lee Dumas
- Mari Smith
- Tom Ziglar
- Ray Edwards

When it comes to LinkedIn, there are pretty much three people I listen to, but only one has ever dropped new business right in my lap the way John Nemo did. You know me. I don't recommend people lightly. John Nemo is worth your time. Jump on this!

Chris Brogan, NYT Bestselling Author & Consultant

John Nemo took my LinkedIn profile page and ignited it in a way I hadn't seen done before. After witnessing John's expertise up close and personal, it's easy to see why he's been crushing it on LinkedIn the past few years. Simply put, when it comes to LinkedIn, John Nemo is the real deal. Can't wait to share more of his LinkedIn knowledge bombs with the rest of Fire Nation soon!

John Lee Dumas, "Entrepreneur on Fire" Podcast

Once John updated and optimized my LinkedIn profile, I immediately (and I mean immediately!) began to see results. From inbound media and interview requests to people asking more about working with Ziglar, it all happened within a few days of John making my updated profile live. I highly encourage you to check out John Nemo and LinkedIn Riches. I know it will make a difference for you just like it has for me!

Tom Ziglar, CEO, Ziglar, Inc.

I don't share all this to brag, but rather to reassure you that your time with me won't be wasted.

What you'll discover in this guide is the EXACT template I use for myself and my clients when it comes to creating a client-attracting LinkedIn profile.

So let's get to it!

Why LinkedIn Matters

With (as of this writing) nearly 900 million members in 200+ countries and territories around the world, and with 2 new members joining every second, LinkedIn is the worlds' largest "one stop shop" for professionals on the planet.

People log into LinkedIn daily to read industry news, get industry-specific training, find their next employee, find a new job, join professional groups to share best practices, network and much more.

And because LinkedIn has gone full "Big Brother" on each of its members, *every* single piece of data a member has ever entered (from his or her profile page content to status updates, etc.) has been sorted, indexed and saved in what amounts to the world's largest internal search engine for B2B leads.

Linked's powerful SEO juice even carries outside the platform as well.

Here's a simple test: Google your name, and chances are excellent your LinkedIn profile will be among the top results.

Which begs the question - what will your ideal clients and prospects see when they land on *your* current LinkedIn profile page?

If you're first reaction to that sentence is sheer panic, don't worry - you're far from alone in having a LinkedIn profile that needs an overhaul.

The Single Biggest Mistake People Make on LinkedIn

In fact, I'd argue that 99 percent of people on LinkedIn are using the platform the wrong way.

Let me explain.

When LinkedIn started back in 2003, the whole idea was to post your résumé online, and maybe an HR person or recruiter would find you on the network. You could also search and apply for jobs through LinkedIn's database.

So all of us did what LinkedIn wanted us to – we generated profiles that were all about … wait for it … ourselves! We posted our résumés and we talked about where we went to college. We talked about our jobs, industry awards we'd won, certifications and more.

Bottom line: We talked about ourselves.

Incessantly.

Think about that.

We've all been at a cocktail party or social gathering and met a guy who literally never stops talking about himself. We might be trapped in a 10-minute conversation with him, and never once does he ask us a question about ourselves or how he can help us out.

That's super annoying, right?

Then why do we do the same thing with our LinkedIn profiles?

I hate to break it to you, but outside of your mom and your dog (cats don't count), nobody really cares all that much about you.

You know what other people do care about?

Themselves!

They care about getting their problems solved. They care about finding a product, service, or person to help them achieve their goals.

Dale Carnegie said it best in his book *How to Win Friends and Influence People:* "I know and you know people who blunder through life trying to wigwag other people into becoming interested in them. Of course, it doesn't work. People are not interested in you. They are not interested in me. They are interested in themselves – morning, noon and after dinner."

That's what I mean when I say 99 percent of people are using LinkedIn the wrong way. They've got profiles that only talk about *themselves.*

So, if you truly want to create a killer LinkedIn profile that attracts clients and generates warm, inbound sales leads, it's critical to stop making this mistake.

The Solution – Create a "Client-Facing" Profile

Instead of having your profile read like an online résumé, you need to make it all about how you can help a specific, targeted audience of customers and clients achieve their goals by utilizing your service or product.

Go back through your LinkedIn profile and try to answer these types of questions:

How is what I'm sharing here going to help my ideal client or customer solve his or her biggest problem?

How is what I'm posting here going to help my ideal client make more money, save time, and solve core challenges I know he or she faces?

It's all about flipping the old, outdated view of LinkedIn being a job seeker/hiring manager network upside down, and instead building a personal brand that makes it clear who you are, what you do, and the unique value or benefit you can bring to a specific audience in the workplace.

Once you have your profile in order, going out on LinkedIn to find, engage, and sell to your ideal clients and customers becomes far easier.

Fix-it-Felix and 1990s Lyrical Poets

Allow me to illustrate.

If you haven't seen the Disney movie *Wreck-It-Ralph*, it's a hilarious, animated throwback to the glory days of 1980s era video games.

If, like me, you grew up during that hilarious decade, you'll instantly be transported back to the days of tube socks pulled up to your knees, short shorts, a fistful of quarters and Ms. Pac-Man, Defender, and Donkey Kong awaiting your best effort at the local video arcade.

Here I was, in fact, at the height of my 1980s glory.

In the image below (I'm on the far left, head in my hands!), my older sisters and I were "enjoying" Disneyworld in the middle of July, when Orlando, Florida, transforms from the "Happiest Place on Earth" into a swampy, burning furnace straight from the fires of hell:

My parents (both teachers) took us to Disney during the Summer break because it was cheaper and easier to get time off … they forgot to mention it would be the kid equivalent to walking on the sun.

Here's the point of my trip down 1980s pop culture memory lane: *Fix-It Felix* is one of the most popular video game characters in *Wreck-It-Ralph*.

Felix is beloved by everyone he encounters, because if anything breaks … he fixes it! Armed with a golden hammer, Felix spends his days fixing his customer's problems. (See where I'm going with this?)

Or, as another late 1980s and early 1990s icon of eloquence put it: "If you got a problem, yo I'll solve it, now check out the moves while my DJ revolves it!"

Ice, Ice, baby.

Yes, Vanilla Ice was a lyrical poet, and Miami was indeed on the scene just in case you didn't know it. But Vanilla and Felix are trying to convey a timeless sales and marketing truth to us: *You must make your LinkedIn profile about the problems you solve for your customers!*

With that in mind, I want you to refocus, repurpose and reframe every sentence of your LinkedIn Profile to answer this question: *How does what I'm saying right now help YOU (my ideal client or customer) make more money or get what you want?*

Now, before you hit the panic button, I want to share some good news: I have scripts for you! They're simple, fill-in-the-blank templates you can utilize like those *Wacky Mad Libs* books – see, I knew I could work in another 1980s reference!

But before we get to those, I want to make sure you understand the key to a client-attracting LinkedIn profile when it comes to the style and tone of the text you use.

Don't Be This Guy (or Gal) on LinkedIn!

I had no idea I was connected to such virtual greatness over on LinkedIn.

Having recently spent a few days sorting through and organizing my 19,753 LinkedIn connections, I discovered I was connected to 229 "Masters," 75 "Gurus," 45 "Ninjas," 15 "Geniuses," 3 "Rock Stars" and even a pair of "Sensei."

Yes, those are real terms and phrases people I'm connected to on LinkedIn use to describe themselves as part of their professional headline.

To quote tennis great John McEnroe during a 1980s (of course!) on court meltdown at an umpire during Wimbledon: *"You cannot be serious!"*

And, while I'm making light of the examples above, they reveal what I believe is the "make or break" section of your entire effort on LinkedIn – your profile headline.

Next to your photo, nothing matters more on LinkedIn than the profile title or headline you use to explain who you are, what you do and the audiences you serve. In fact, it follows you everywhere you go on the platform, always appearing right below your name and photo on the site.

Clever vs. Clear

Yet far too many examples exist (in my own network, and likely in yours as well) of professionals trying to be "unique" or stand out from the crowd by writing clever or cute descriptions of a service they offer that also conveys a sense of authority, such as "Lead Generation Ninja."

In this example, of course, the person is offering Lead Generation as a service, and is *claiming* authority and expertise by calling himself a "Ninja."

In reality, *calling* yourself an expert (no matter how cool-sounding or hip the word choice) doesn't actually *make* you one.

We live in a "prove it" era of online marketing, one where talk is cheap. Instead, if you want to actually have people hire you to generate leads for them with LinkedIn, you must first *demonstrate* expertise and authority through the content you create, the advice you give and so on.

Yes, you can still leverage trusted authority markers like media appearances, awards you've won and so on, but those can be hard to jam into a LinkedIn profile headline.

So, instead of trying to be *clever* with your LinkedIn headline, be *clear* instead.

The idea is for someone to understand within a few seconds *what* you do and *who* you do it for.

The Ideal LinkedIn Profile Headline Formula

Here's a simple formula you can use to craft a client-attracting LinkedIn profile headline:

Service I Provide + Target Audience(s) I Serve

Here's how it looks in action:

John Nemo

"Done For You" LinkedIn Lead Generation for Business Coaches, Consultants & Small Business Owners

The "service" I offer is DFY LinkedIn Lead Generation. The "target audiences" I offer it to are Business Coaches, Consultants & Small Business Owners.

Here's an example of a client of ours (Tracy Paukstys):

Tracy Murphy Paukstys, PCC, CPC, ELI-MP

1st

Leadership Development + Executive Coaching for Fortune 500
Clients | Serving Marketing, Insights & Analytics Leadership

Tracy is an Executive Coach with an incredible list of big-name clients to her name. So we want to make it clear *what* she does and *who* she serves in her LinkedIn headline.

Have a look at Kathryn Bishop, another client who provides Accounting, Bookkeeping and CPA services:

Kathryn J. Bishop CPA · 1st

Construction Accounting & Bookkeeping 👷 Construction Payroll & Taxes 🚧 Job Costing + Cash Flow Analysis

Along with sharing her services, we hyper-niched Kathryn to a specific target audience (Construction) - more on this later.

Another example from our client Pete Poggi:

Pete Poggi · 1st

Insurance Agency Franchising & Training For Licensed Florida
Insurance Agents Who Want To Grow A Successful Agency

If you're an insurance agent in Florida, you know within moments why you might want to connect with Pete and what's in it for you, right?

One last example from our client Alan Gentry, who owns a product-based business:

Alan Gentry · 1st

Print Design ✍ + Print Production 👕 + Apparel Sourcing 🧵
Creating all-in-one, full-package custom t-shirts for Fortune 500
companies like Coca-Cola, adidas, and McDonalds

Alan has an incredible apparel company and caters to big-name clients - again, within seconds of seeing his profile headline you know *what* he does and *who* it's for.

Don't overthink this – keep your LinkedIn profile headline simple and clear, remembering that we live in a hyper-fast, Google-ized world where people expect instant, easy and simple-to-digest information online.

If you take this approach on LinkedIn and kick your inner Ninja and Guru self to the curb, you'll get much better results on the world's largest platform for professionals.

Bonus Tip - LinkedIn Keywords

When you're looking for the *"Service I Provide"* part of your LinkedIn headline formula, use the keywords that LinkedIn "likes" for its platform.

Here's how to figure that out: If you navigate to the "Skills" section of your own LinkedIn profile, you'll see the ability to "add a skill" and then a drop down menu that appears once you start typing a "skill" (i.e. a keyword).

Here's what the "Skills" section looks like on your profile page:

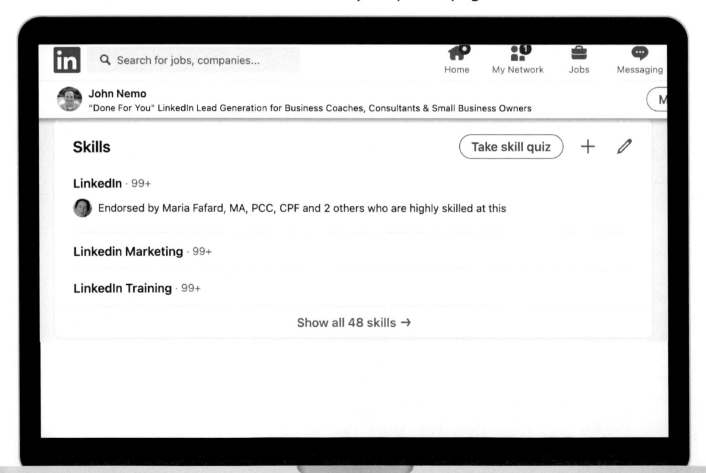

Once you find that section on your profile page, click the "+" symbol to get to the area where you can add new skills:

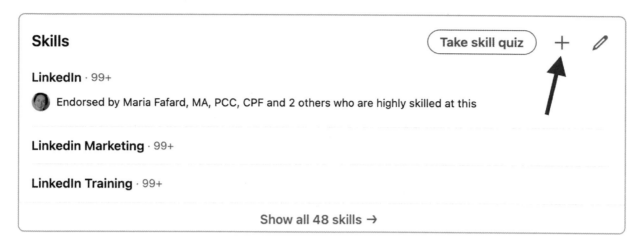

Next click "Add Another Skill":

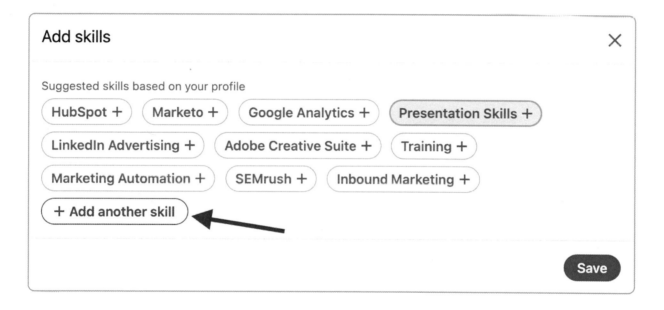

Now start typing in the keyword or phrase you want to test:

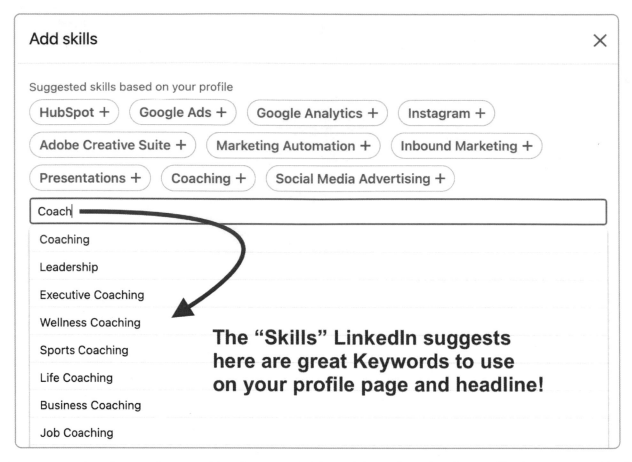

In the example above, I typed in the word "Coach" and LinkedIn pulled up several "skills" related to that phrase.

You can see how using "skills" like "Executive Coaching" or "Business Coaching" are not only great / simple ways to explain what you do in a LinkedIn headline - they're also "keyword friendly" and "liked" by LinkedIn's internal search engine, since it *wants* you to list those phrases on your profile as "skills" you have.

Remember, LinkedIn is a giant *search engine* - every piece of content you publish is saved, sorted and indexed so other people can search for it.

So by using LinkedIn's suggested keywords / skills, you're making it easier for your ideal prospects to "find" you on the platform.

With LinkedIn, The Riches Are In The Niches!

Also, as I alluded to before, the more niche you can get with your approach on LinkedIn, the more successful you'll become.

I'll show you later on how to appeal to multiple audiences or multiple niches on LinkedIn, so don't worry that you're somehow going to have to limit yourself in the process.

The key is making it clear, simple and fast for people to decipher who you are, the audience you serve and the product or service you provide.

Remember: You can't succeed on LinkedIn trying to be everything to everyone. Instead, you must define a few niche, target audiences to appeal to, and then build outward from there.

Bottom line: *If you try to be everything to everyone on LinkedIn, you'll be nothing to noone.*

LinkedIn Header Artwork - Social Proof or Topic-Based

Behind your smiling face on your LinkedIn profile is page your "header image" area.

This essentially services as a visual "billboard" to give people a quick idea of what you're all about.

The best use of this space is NOT a nature scene, photo quote or your company logo!

Instead, use it one of two ways:

Option 1: *Social Proof + Service Your Provide*

Option 2: *Topic + Service You Provide*

Here's an example of of a client of ours (Libby Gill) who has a ton of social proof based on media interviews:

Note that along with "Where You've Seen Me" and the media logos, we *also* have the text "Executive Coach | Leadership Expert | Award-Winning Author" as well.

Social Proof (media logos) + Service Libby provides (Executive Coach)

Here's a "topic" based example from our client Kathryn Bishop:

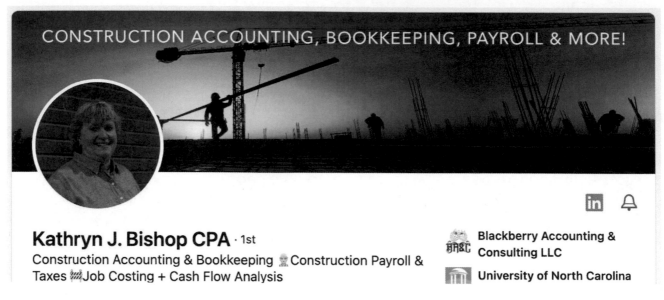

Note the "visual" theme/topic of Kathryn's audience - Construction.

And then she has the words "Construction Accounting, Bookkeeping, Payroll & More!" to help illustrate the service she provides.

In the case of Alan Gentry's LinkedIn header image, we're showcasing his product:

For our client Tracy we're using the social proof of her big-name client roster along with the service she provides (Leadership Development & Executive Coaching):

See how simple, clear and visually appealing those headers are?

Your LinkedIn About Section - Where The Action Starts!

Now that we've got your LinkedIn profile headline and visual header in place, let's get to your "About" section.

Again, this is where *most* LinkedIn profiles go the wrong way - people talk about themselves in the third person, like they're a pro athlete or celebrity, bragging about their work accomplishments and so on.

Again, nobody cares!

Instead, you need to flip the script and make this area "client facing!"

Here's a simple template you can fill in the blanks with to accomplish it:

WHAT I DO: *I help [MY TARGET AUDIENCE] achieve [THEIR GOAL] by providing [MY PRODUCT/SERVICE].*

WHERE YOU'VE SEEN ME: *[INSERT BULLETED "EMOJI" LIST OF MEDIA LOGOS or BIG-NAME CLIENT LOGO]*

WHERE YOU'VE SEEN MY WORK: *[INSERT BULLETED "EMOJI" LIST OF MEDIA LOGOS]*

WHO I WORK WITH: *I partner with [TARGET AUDIENCE or INDUSTRY TYPE] including:*

[INSERT BULLETED "EMOJI" LIST OF JOB TITLES, INDUSTRY NAMES, etc.]

SERVICES I PROVIDE: *[INSERT BULLETED "EMOJI" LIST OF SERVICES YOU PROVIDE, etc.]*

WHAT MAKES ME UNIQUE: *[Answer that question! What makes you unique/different/better than your competitors? XYZ years of experience? Certifications/ Patents/etc.? Personal, 1-on-1 attention and Customer Service/ Support?]*

WHAT OTHERS SAY:
[COPY AND PASTE IN 2-3 TESTIMONIALS IN THIS AREA. USE A REAL PERSON, FULL NAME, COMPANY NAME, ETC. AND EXPLAIN SPECIFIC VALUE/BENEFIT PERSON RECEIVED FROM YOU OR YOUR BUSINESS.]

READY TO TALK? *Reach out to me directly here on LinkedIn or [visit me online at URL or email me at XYZ or call me directly at XYZ].*

Let's break down how this template works.

First off, using ALL CAPS phrases like "WHAT I DO" or "WHAT MAKES ME UNIQUE" helps call attention to key parts of your profile.

Next, you can *rearrange* the sections of the template above depending on what is *most* intriguing / interesting / important / unique about your specific situation.

For instance, if you've got big-name clients, put that toward the top in the "WHERE YOU'VE SEEN MY WORK" list.

If the real "hook" about you is the unique backstory / compelling professional background you have had, move that up higher with the "WHAT MAKES ME UNIQUE" section.

If you've got glowing testimonials from big-name clients in your niche, move the "WHAT OTHERS SAY" section up higher.

I always like to keep "WHAT I DO" as the first sentence of your "About" section, simply because that helps people know within a few seconds *what* you do, *who* it's for and *why* they should care (the benefit they get).

After that, I typically will reorder the other template sections based on our client and his or her situation.

Add Some Visual Sizzle!

Also, I use the website getemoji.com to find emojis to use instead of boring old bullet points.

As you'll see in the examples below, adding emojis in a *tasteful* fashion brings some much-needed visual sizzle to your LinkedIn profile and helps break up long blocks of text or lists with creative visual cues.

If you're not familiar with how this works, go to the "Get Emoji" website and just copy/paste an emoji from it like you copy/paste text.

Use an emoji where you'd normally put a bullet point or a dash when compiling a list.

For example, you can use these types of emojis when doing a list of media credits:

WHERE YOU'VE SEEN ME:
- CNN
- The New York Times
- NPR
- The Wall Street Journal

Last thing: If you think emojis are "unprofessional" … may I politely suggest you get over yourself!

They are a fun, creative and (most important!) *visual* way to communicate that goes beyond boring, bland text.

Remember, the way people read online is by *scanning*. We race up or down a feed or screen, and what "stops" our scroll is visuals or ALL CAPS HEADLINES or something else.

Big, boring blocks of text without much white space between will get glossed over or skipped by your average online reader.

That's not to say that you can't overdo it with emojis or use them in poor taste. Keep them professional and relevant to the text you want to enhance. Also, "less is more" is a good rule to follow with emojis and your LinkedIn profile.

And, if you're just not comfortable with emojis, skip them - life will go on!

What a Client-Attracting "About" Section Looks Like

With that in mind, let's have a look at some examples of a LinkedIn profile's "About" section.

Let's start with Libby Gill, who has both big-name clients *and* big-name media interviews to lean on:

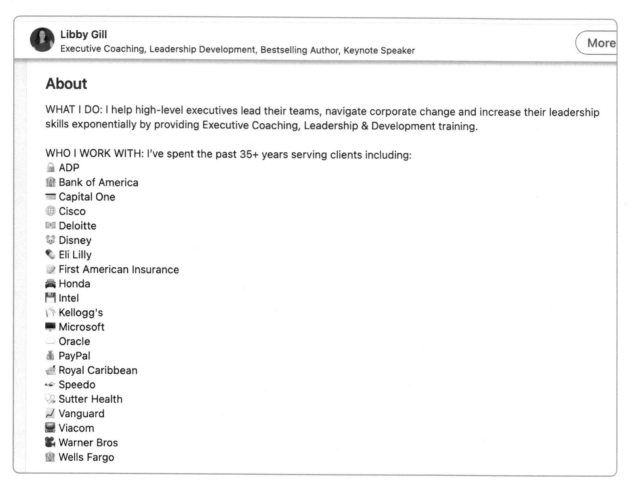

See how we start Libby's "About" section with "WHAT I DO" and then pivot to the big-name clients in "WHO I WORK WITH"?

Next up we hit on her social proof in terms of media with "WHERE YOU'VE SEEN ME" and then get into "TOPICS I COVER" (the services she provides" and testimonials "WHAT OTHERS SAY" –

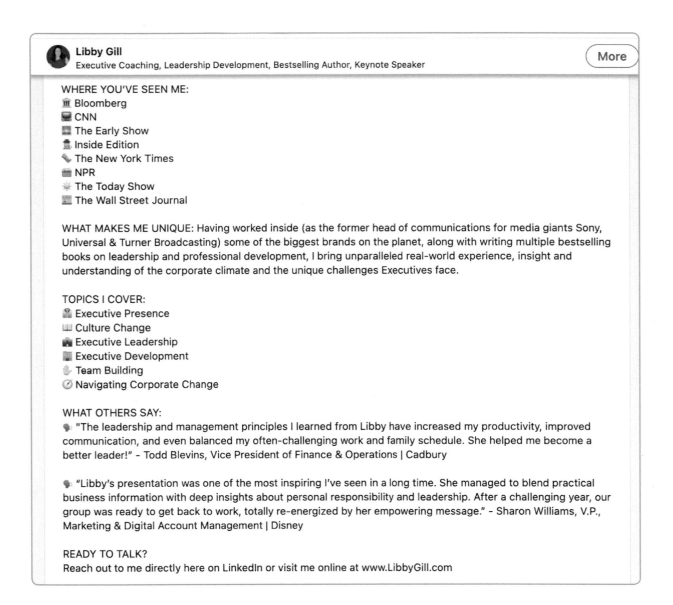

Libby Gill
Executive Coaching, Leadership Development, Bestselling Author, Keynote Speaker

More

WHERE YOU'VE SEEN ME:
- Bloomberg
- CNN
- The Early Show
- Inside Edition
- The New York Times
- NPR
- The Today Show
- The Wall Street Journal

WHAT MAKES ME UNIQUE: Having worked inside (as the former head of communications for media giants Sony, Universal & Turner Broadcasting) some of the biggest brands on the planet, along with writing multiple bestselling books on leadership and professional development, I bring unparalleled real-world experience, insight and understanding of the corporate climate and the unique challenges Executives face.

TOPICS I COVER:
- Executive Presence
- Culture Change
- Executive Leadership
- Executive Development
- Team Building
- Navigating Corporate Change

WHAT OTHERS SAY:
"The leadership and management principles I learned from Libby have increased my productivity, improved communication, and even balanced my often-challenging work and family schedule. She helped me become a better leader!" - Todd Blevins, Vice President of Finance & Operations | Cadbury

"Libby's presentation was one of the most inspiring I've seen in a long time. She managed to blend practical business information with deep insights about personal responsibility and leadership. After a challenging year, our group was ready to get back to work, totally re-energized by her empowering message." - Sharon Williams, V.P., Marketing & Digital Account Management | Disney

READY TO TALK?
Reach out to me directly here on LinkedIn or visit me online at www.LibbyGill.com

With our client Kathryn Bishop, she didn't have big-name clients or media accolades.

So we led instead with "WHAT MAKES ME UNIQUE" along with a hyper-niche focus (remember, the riches are in the niches!) on a target audience:

Kathryn J. Bishop CPA

Construction Accounting & Bookkeeping 👷Construction Payroll & Taxes 🏗Job Costing + Cash Flow Analysis

More

About

🏗WHAT I DO: I help Contractors in the Construction industry & Homebuilders boost their profits, improve cash flow, and run a tight financial ship by using my 20+ years of experience as a CPA doing accounting, bookkeeping, and acting as a Controller.

🏢WHAT MAKES ME UNIQUE: I've got "Big Firm" experience having worked at Deloitte and at Duke Energy, where I implemented projects that saved the company $300 million over 10 years' time. I've even taught accounting at the college level. Plus, I'm a CPA and have a Master's in Accounting.

👷INDUSTRY EXPERTISE: My Dad was a Contractor and my Mom a CPA (a match made in heaven!). So I LITERALLY grew up in the construction industry, having to be on the job site each Saturday by 8 a.m. growing up.

As a result, I have unparalleled insight into and expertise around the unique dynamics running your own contracting or construction business, the role your family plays and much more.

SERVICES I PROVIDE:
📋Accounts Payable & Accounts Receivable
📊Cash Flow Analysis
🏗Construction Accounting
🏢Construction Bookkeeping
📊Construction Cost Control + Job Costing
🔍Financial Reviews
🧾Income Taxes
💰Payroll Taxes
👩Virtual CFO & Controller

🎤HOW IT WORKS: Everything starts with a conversation. As a warning, I like stories and I'm Southern, so be prepared to tell me all about your business plans, personal goals, family, pets, hobbies, & favorite vacation spots! 😊

Note how we used construction emojis and led with "WHAT MAKES ME UNIQUE" and "INDUSTRY EXPERIENCE" to help set Kathryn apart from the competition.

Because Kathryn literally *grew up* in the Construction industry, along with a mom who was a CPA, plus her "big firm" experience but "small firm" customer service, if you're a construction professional, who better to do your books?

With the rest of Kathryn's profile we get deeper into the services she provides (again note the "construction" themed emojis!) and her unique style / approach to customer service:

Kathryn J. Bishop CPA
Construction Accounting & Bookkeeping 🏗Construction Payroll & Taxes 📊Job Costing + Cash Flow Analysis

More

SERVICES I PROVIDE:
📋Accounts Payable & Accounts Receivable
💵Cash Flow Analysis
📊Construction Accounting
📒Construction Bookkeeping
📊Construction Cost Control + Job Costing
🔍Financial Reviews
🏦Income Taxes
💰Payroll Taxes
👩‍💼Virtual CFO & Controller

📢HOW IT WORKS: Everything starts with a conversation. As a warning, I like stories and I'm Southern, so be prepared to tell me all about your business plans, personal goals, family, pets, hobbies, & favorite vacation spots! 😊

MY STYLE: I'm an informal person by nature, but I am also VERY good at what I do. Once I understand what you want out of life, I will analyze where you are and together we'll work to get you there. I am also very confident that I can explain complex accounting principles in plain English. Trust me on this, if I can pitch a $3M system improvement idea to a CFO in a timed seven minute presentation, I can answer any questions you might have about your books!

📞 READY TO TALK?
Connect with me here on LinkedIn, visit my website at https://www.blackberryacct.com or just call me at 704-965-7433

📋AREAS OF EXPERTISE: Construction Accounting | Construction Cost Control | Part-Time CFO Services | Construction Estimating | Payroll Taxes | CFO | Bookkeeping | Construction | Financial Accounting | Accounts Payable & Receivable | Accounts Receivable (AR) | Tax Preparation | Tax Accounting | Tax Advisory | Tax Compliance | Accounting | Construction Administration Services

Bonus Tip - Repurpose Your "About" Section in the "Experience" Area

An easy way to ensure your amazing "About" section doesn't get missed by someone viewing your LinkedIn profile is to copy and paste its contents into your first position / job listing in the "Experience" section of your LinkedIn profile.

Here's an example of this using Kathryn Bishop's profile:

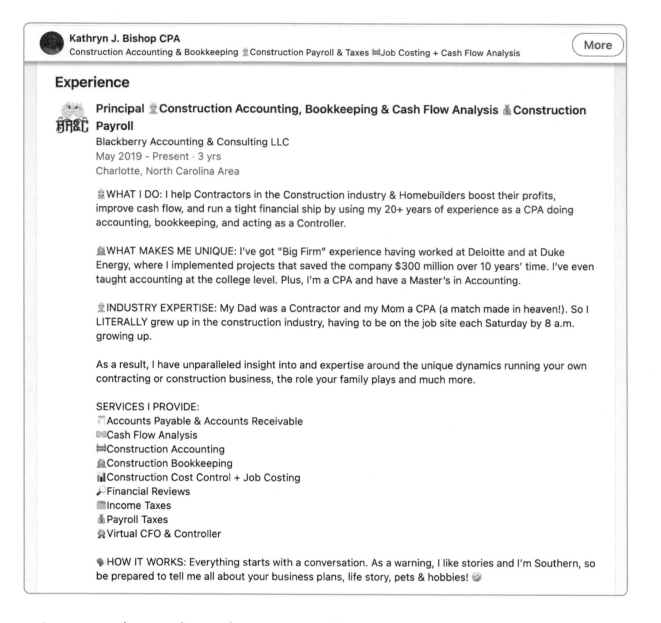

Sometimes people can skip right past your "About" section and start with your "Experience" area, so make sure your first job listing reflects what you had in the "About" section!

How To Appeal To Multiple Audiences on LinkedIn

Obviously with your LinkedIn headline and "About" section you can try and appeal to 1, 2 or at most 3 different target audiences, but what about going deeper?

What if you have multiple audiences, multiple products and services?

No worries - just create additional "positions" under a company name in your Experience section:

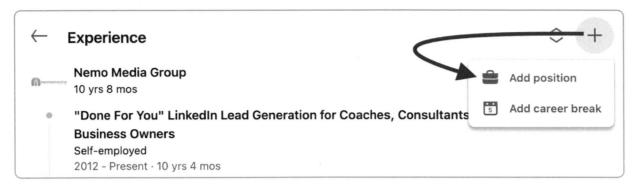

Here's an example of how in my "Experience" section I list one company (Nemo Media Group) but then add multiple "positions" to cover the different services I offer:

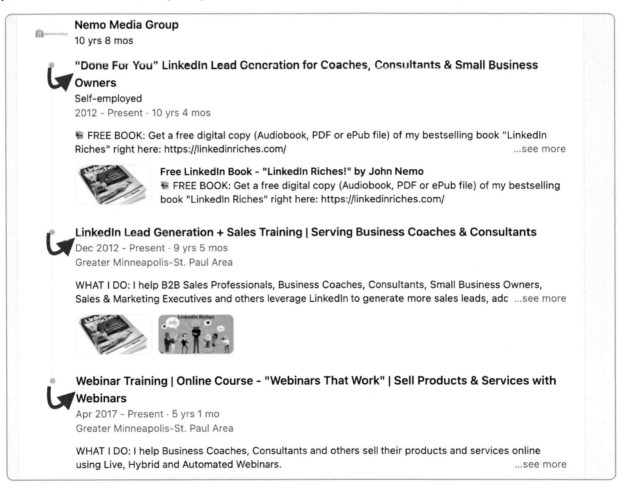

I actually have five MORE "positions" under the Nemo Media Group listing, including 1-on-1 Coaching, Keynote Speaker, other online courses, etc.

With each "position" you list, you can go more in-depth about that specific line of service, product, etc., as needed.

Let's Do This!

Of course, there are many more (smaller) pieces to crafting a client-attracting LinkedIn profile, but this free template has given you the big (and key!) elements to update if you want to turn prospects visiting your profile into paying clients.

So get after it!

Next Steps - Let's Connect!

Reach out and invite me to connect over on LinkedIn!

Make sure you include a personal note letting me know you read this guide and wanted to connect as a result.

I can't wait to see your updated profile!

Free Resources

If you want some additional tips on how to craft a client-attracting LinkedIn profile + discover how to generate nonstop leads on the platform, grab a free digital copy (Audiobook, PDF or ePub file) of my bestselling book "LinkedIn Riches: How To Use LinkedIn for Business, Sales and Marketing!"

Click the image below or go to https://linkedinriches.com/ to grab your copy.

You can also go to https://linkedinriches.com/free/ to watch free on-demand training videos and replays of my "Noon With Nemo" live sessions.

Done For You Help

If you'd like my agency (Nemo Media Group) to rewrite your LinkedIn profile *for* you and/or generate leads for your business, let's talk!

Visit us online at https://nemomediagroup.com/ or click the image below to start the conversation!

Please note: There's no pressure or heavy-handed sales pitch involved.

Rather, we need to learn a bit more about your and your unique situation, target audience, etc., so we can (A) see if you'd be a good fit for our DFY program and (B) bring you any specific ideas or insights based on the information you share.

Online Courses

I've got multiple online courses on everything from LinkedIn lead generation to selling your products or services with webinars to podcasting to mindset and much more.

Visit https://nemomediagroup.com/online-courses/ to see a list of current courses.

About The Author

John Nemo is the Founder and CEO of Nemo Media Group, a LinkedIn lead generation and digital marketing agency based in Minneapolis, Minnesota.

John is also an Online Course Creator and Bestselling Author who helps Business Coaches, Consultants, Entrepreneurs and Small Business Owners generate quality leads, build their client base and increase revenue using digital marketing platforms, tools and strategies like Content Marketing, LinkedIn and Webinars.

The author of 8 books, John is a former Associated Press Reporter, Talk Radio Producer, Award-Winning PR Director and Social Media Consultant based in Minneapolis, Minnesota.

John has personally rewritten LinkedIn profiles for A-List Entrepreneurs, Speakers and Bestselling Authors including Chris Brogan, Mari Smith, John Lee Dumas, Bob Burg, Tom Ziglar, Jairek Robbins, Dan Miller, Ray Edwards and many others.

In addition, John regularly guest blogs for *Inc. Magazine* and *American City Business Journals*, and his work has also been featured in *The Huffington Post, Business Insider*, on LinkedIn's official marketing blog, the *Entrepreneur On Fire* and *Social Media Examiner* podcasts and many other outlets online.

Since 2012, John has helped hundreds of Business Coaches, Consultants, Small Business Owners, Entrepreneurs and others across dozens of different industries worldwide leverage LinkedIn to generate nonstop sales leads, clients and revenue.

The son of two English teachers, John grew up in a home where the basement walls were lined floor-to-ceiling with books. A lifelong love of story led him to a career in journalism, where he started his career in 1997 as a reporter for *The Arizona Republic* and later the Associated Press.

John later worked in talk radio as a producer and on-air talent at *KTIS-AM* radio in Minneapolis-St. Paul. He also served as a freelance writer for hundreds of different magazines, newspapers and websites, covering topics ranging from Fantasy Football to Norwegian Architecture to Rock Music.

John has also worked as a national-award winning PR and Social Media Director for large trade associations in the debt collection and healthcare industries.

During its first 90 days, his 2009 PR campaign for the consumer financial education website Ask Doctor Debt led to more than 125 interviews across the United States, reaching an estimated 25 million consumers and netting an estimated $1 million in free advertising/publicity value. John was also able to secure a weekly, ongoing segment for Ask Doctor Debt and ACA International representatives on top-rated Fox News Channel that ran weekly for more than four months straight.

In 2010, John's PR campaign for the Minnesota Nurses Association (MNA) reached an estimated 133 million people in just 90 days and would have cost $5 million in advertising costs to duplicate. Billed as the largest nurses' strike in U.S. history, John's campaign garnered local, national and international media coverage from outlets as far away as BBC Radio in London.

During those same 90 days, John created and executed a Social Media Campaign for MNA that took its Facebook page from 0 to 11,000 fans, racking up 496,000 views. He also created and distributed content through an MNA Blog that generated 342,000 page views and 2,800 comments, along with building a YouTube channel that generated 97,000 views.

In the summer of 2011, John helped create and release the Minnesota Nurses Association iPhone/iPad App, which made MNA one of the first Labor Unions in the United States to release its own App. It allowed MNA's 20,000 members to get the latest association news, videos and updates, report unsafe staffing at their hospitals, look up and contact their local legislators and more.

In 2012, John Nemo left MNA to start his own marketing agency, Nemo Media Group, which provided services including Consulting, Website Design, Copywriting, Video Marketing, Social Media Marketing, Content Creation, Sales Presentations and more for clients across the United States.

In 2014, John created his first online course, LinkedIn Riches, followed by Webinars That Work and Content Marketing Machine.

John lives in Minneapolis, Minnesota with his wife, Sara, their three crazy young boys and Rosie the dog.

Bonus / fun fact: You can use the website https://turnedyellow.com/ to turn a family photo into characters from *The Simpsons* like I did with our family:

Yes!

I knew I could work in one last 1980s reference - *The Simpsons* started in 1989.

My work here is done!

Made in United States
Orlando, FL
13 September 2022